Family & Community History

Alice's Family Album

Alice's Family Album

Alice's Family Album

With Memories of Don Thompson Vocational School

Alice Moore

Memoir, Local History
Alice's Family Album

ISBN: 978-1-966013-03-7 Soft cover
Publisher's note: We decided to enlarge and repeat similar photos in hopes that details missed by most might
be the missing link for a researcher seeking a house that no longer exists or wanting to learn more about a
once-standing place or item. We hope you find it. The photos included, from the author's personal collection,
could have been lost forever. Thank you, Alice, for sharing them with us.

Published January 2026 by Sula Too Publishing, Tampa, Florida.
Printed in the United States.

Dedicated to:

James Henry Moore
Mary Elizabeth Moore
Grandchildren: Javari Moore, Yeshi Moore, Gerrod Moore,
Dekennon Moore, Javia Young, Kevin Young, Jr; Davaris
Moore, Tcendrick Moore
Cousins: Gretta Lumpkin and Dale Horton

Thankyou:

Harriet Scott (inspiration for historic marker),
Francis Jennings for trades and marker support,
Sandy Wright for the memories, and Ersula Odom
for the idea and inspiration.

Table of Contents

Early Childhood

Alice

Alice Moore, age 4, sits holding a cat while gazing into Mrs. Alexander's goldfish pond. The idea that cats dislike water must be true—why else could the three of us exist peacefully? Mrs. Alexander lived next door on Morgan Street, across from Don Thompson. Her house was separated from the school by an alley that seemed to have a life of its own. Mrs. Alexander had cats, and one of the cats I was holding seemed to just take a liking to me, so it became one of my favorites. Whenever I visited, I always looked for that one.

What I find interesting is that the cat didn't try to catch the fish. I have no idea why they don't, or why they didn't. I just sent my girlfriend something about animals because she's going through a stressful time, and I told her that the squirrel and I sit and stare at each other. I don't know why it becomes the fence when I decide not to see it on the patio, and we sit and stare at each other. When I bought the potted plant for the center, I had two—one that Ray brought me, so it's sitting there —and I had to put another in the corner because Brown is in heaven. I had to sit there with another partner, and she came by. Usually, she's on the fence, but she jumped down, looked at the plant, looked around, and I said she looked at me as if to say, "When did you get this?" She sniffed around it, entered the big room, came out, looked at me again, and then went back on the fence. We watched each other, but it was like, "When did you get this?" Then she checked it out. I'm not sure if it's the same one I saw planting a peanut by my glass sliding door.

I have a picture of her sitting on the patio with a peanut. I keep saying she; I don't know if it's a she or a he, but it had a peanut. So I said, "Well, she's going to sit there." Then she went to the fence, and I said she was going to eat that.

She jumped down and came to where I'm sitting by the glass sliding door. You know how the rod slides back when you open it? I was thinking maybe she's up there eating the peanut, but I couldn't imagine her up there. I watched her take that peanut and put it in the groove. It fit perfectly and didn't fall; it stayed there for a few days.

I thought she was eating, but she was actually fixing something inside. After a few days, she went back and retrieved it. You could slide the glass door, and whatever was there— it was just funny to see. So I told her, since she's going through some things, "Why don't you take a walk, sit, and watch the animals? They'll make you laugh. Just watch the clouds." I don't know how she knows that when I come out there, she should get on the fence near me.

My Mom
Mary Moore

Mom and I were very close, and I always remember her making sure I was dressed and ready. She took me everywhere—meetings, church—and we always knew how to dress well. We attended all the meetings and church, and I remember us together in Sunday school. When we moved to West Tampa, she signed me up for tap

dance classes at the Kid Mason Center. Later, she had me take piano lessons just a block away, so I wouldn't have to go far. As I grew older, she also taught me to cook because she was a very good cook. However, she refused to cook chitlins—she considered that a no-no.

My dad would go to Roger's Dining Room on Central Avenue for his plate of chitlins, but that was never her thing. If he went, she and I would sit in the car on Central, and she would always tell him to park properly so we could see the people.

Mom and I would get food from Cozy Corner. We sat in the car, watching people go up and down Central Avenue for parties and other events. She enjoyed doing that, and there was never an argument about him going to the restaurant or The Cotton Club. That was his thing — they were always together.

As time went on, we moved to West Tampa, and they purchased a house with an adjoining store and named it *Mary's Groceries*. Mom worked in the store and my job, during the summer, was to run errands for her. This included walking three blocks to Alessi Bakery to purchase Cuban bread for the sandwiches she made. At that time, Alessi Bakery was on Chestnut and Howard. The great thing about family-run places like that was that everyone knew you when you walked in, they were friendly, and it was safe.

Mom's sandwiches were favorites of the Southern Cross Mattress Factory employees and the neighborhood. We live across the street from the factory.

Mom and Mary's Groceries also sold cookies, candies, and soda water. Our store was located at Rome and Chestnut, near the railroad tracks. Since it was my family's store, I could get anything I wanted.

When I had my daughter, Mom was very kind and stayed home. My friends would come over, and she would make us feel very comfortable by watching "the stories" (soap operas) and wearing knee-high socks, just sitting and enjoying our time together at home. Many times, including when I graduated from high school, a classmate threw a party. Mom went with me to friend's graduation party. Even though she did not drink, I insisted that she have a drink. That wasn't her thing, but she had one.

Still, we were very close; she kept many things to herself and didn't discuss everything, but I really enjoyed being with her. We truly had a lovely time, and she tried to introduce me to the best things, including Kid Mason's tap-dancing classes.

I also became a member of the NAACP during Saunders's tenure. These small experiences, I suppose, are why I am so outgoing and involved in community service. That was my background. Even with the clubs she was part of, I recall the TVs they used to raise money for various causes.

The other women I spent time with at their homes made those moments even more enjoyable. I don't remember exactly how I met the Claxtons, but when the Florida State Fair time came around, they would stay at their house in West Tampa. He had two daughters, one named Olivia. I loved visiting them and playing downstairs—the only place I knew with a basement.

Sometimes they would come and stay, and we'd have a great time socializing. We would accompany her to various social club events. To this day, I don't know the names of these clubs; I've never heard them mentioned. Mrs. Wade owned a racehorse and would come to town during horse racing season. After her husband died, she continued attending her clubs, and every year she hosted meetings—sometimes at her house on the corner of Scott or Morgan, though I forget the street. Mrs. Wade was the only person I saw with a chauffeur, and I was amazed by that. I still laugh when I think about how, during their meetings, they would let me serve the china and silverware, which I found funny. She kept her husband's ashes in a special spot in the apartment.

State Board for Vocational Education

TRADE AND INDUSTRIAL DIVISION

This is to Certify that __Mary Moore__

has satisfactorily completed a Unit Course in __Elementary Foods__

relating to __Household Employment__ at __Longview__

covering __100__ hours from __10/9__ 19 __39__ to __4/8__ 19 __40__

H. L. Foster
City Superintendent of Schools
City Director of Industrial Education

Unit Course No. __HE-3__

James R. D. Eddy
State Director of Industrial
Education

E. B. Pigford
Teacher

Issued at Austin, Texas, __5/14__ 19 __40__.

S507-440-5M

This is my mom's certificate, showing she graduated, though she says it's from a cooking class. I know there's another term for it, but she was a really good cook. When we moved to West Tampa, she opened a store, or I should say, we opened the store—she and Daddy. She cooked for the Southern Cross Mattress Factory, and many people enjoyed her oatmeal cookies. I still meet folks today who remember her cookies, like a gentleman who works for the cruise line and an instructor who lived two blocks away. He laughed and said he always remembers her cookies. People loved her food and sandwiches too. Next to the Southern Cross was a feed company, though I can't remember its name. This certificate highlights one of her many skills, confirming that she completed the training and knew what she was doing. The feed store was across the street from the Zansebar Bar on Rome.

Here I am playing in the yard, with some neighboring houses visible in the background. It reminded me of Mrs. Lara, who always kept her yard messy in a creepier way. This shows what Morgan St. looked like and how large the yards were — those yards were quite spacious back then. Still, I can't help but think of Mrs. Lara and her spooky yard, which we used to pass as little girls.

I also remember my mom watching over me, making sure I didn't drive into the street but stayed on the sidewalk. So, I had to stay in the yard. My mother, Mary, was always watching, making sure I stayed safe and didn't venture into the busy yard or street because she wanted to protect me.

Some of my favorite dishes she prepared came from the store. One was the Cuban sandwiches she used to make at home, and I excel at cooking vegetables. The other was the collard greens she would prepare, and I still have the last recipe. But, yes, I think oxtails were the only food I considered art. She was almost a gourmet cook, and most of the time, I have to say, I am too. However, she really had talent and let me help in the kitchen.

I remember a cornbread called hot-water cornbread—I'm not sure if they still call it that— which she always made with greens, cabbage, and green beans. I recall her always telling me to make sure to get the water-ground meal; it had to be water-ground in order to be cooked with hot water and fried. I can't make that anymore. The technique is lost.

I also learned about the pronto pups at the fair, which she always made sure I had. Of course, they don't call them pronto pups anymore; I think they call them corndogs now. The thing is, we actually had the sandwiches she would make to sell. There's not really any dessert I remember her fixing that didn't involve baking. I wouldn't say that was her style; she just didn't do it. But she was always a good cook, and everyone enjoyed whatever she made. I guess part of that is because my children and grandchildren enjoy my cooking, too. My grandson said I made a certain type of rice he remembers to this day. My daughter still remembers the crab enchiladas I made using my mom's recipe. Everybody loved them.

The crab enchilada is made with crab meat, and back then, it was best to use fresh crabs. It includes crab meat, shrimp, bell peppers, onions, sausage, and, of course, Old Bay seasoning, along with very spicy fresh garlic, which made it quite hot. I like it really spicy, though most people don't. Still, everyone loves it. When my daughter got older, she would tell her friends about it, and they wanted me to make it for them. My mom used to make macaroni and cheese — I still love old-fashioned baked macaroni and cheese with a crispy top, not too creamy. I remember her making it, and everyone loved it, so I was glad she did. When my oldest son returned home after 20 years, he thought that I couldn't make it, but I did. We also used to have meatballs, which I prepared for my grandchildren.

My granddaughter remembers them more than anything because they come from my mom's recipe, her great-grandmother's. Even though she was in her 30s or 40s, she kept asking when I would make those meatballs again. Then there were the vegetables, which Mom always cooked with ham hock—that was the only seasoning she used; no other seasonings or smoked foods, as she never used any. I don't either, even now. She also made Cuban sandwiches that everyone in the neighborhood loved whenever she made them. I don't know what was particularly special about how she made them, but people still talk about those sandwiches.

The reason Mom is so skilled in the kitchen is that she has a natural talent, thanks to attending cooking school, and I believe that trait runs in the family. Several cousins, my daughter, and my granddaughters are all very good cooks. My granddaughter is a manager with Aramark. My son cooks very well and wants to open a restaurant, so I think it must be in the DNA, shaped by her training and family. Yes, I can still cook when needed, too. However, I'm more of a gourmet cook than anything else, and everything I know comes from Mom and her training in cooking school at the time.

My Dad
James Henry Moore

This is me, my daddy, James Henry Moore. We went everywhere. He and I were always together. I have fond memories him standing on top of the car at the airport. I used to be able to watch the planes take off, and there was no area where you couldn't stand. That was the part of Boy Scout area that used to be Columbus Drive. Daddy never left me home, nor did Mommy.

We visited many cities in Florida, so it could be almost anywhere. One of their main reasons for moving to Florida was to explore different cities. I enjoyed it because it meant I was constantly traveling. I guess that's why I never learned how to stay home. They were always gone and taking trips around Florida. Traveling is still in my blood.

MOORE, MR. JAMES H. — Mr. James H. Moore, 1714 Chestnut St., passed away July 1, 1979 at his residence. Funeral service will be conducted Saturday at 2:00 PM at the Shady Grove Cemetery with the Rev. L. B. Brown, officiating. A native of Longview, Texas, Mr. Moore had resided in Tampa for several years. He was a graduate of Prarie View A&M University, and a former Welding Instructor at Florida A&M University. Mr. Moore was retired from the Hillsborough County School Board last assigned as a Automotive Mechanics Instructor at Don Thompson Sr., Vocational High School. Survivors include a devoted daughter, Ms. Alice Moore of Tampa; two brothers, Mr. Willie

Don Thompson

A black-and-white photo of Don Thompson Vocational School in Tampa shows several staff members standing in front (from left to right: Lee Davis, Mrs. Davis G.D. Rogers, Mr. Bosbo, and two others, with a bus used for "free health checks." HCPL

History of Don Thompson: In 1945, Don Thompson Vocational High School opened on Morgan Street in Tampa, primarily serving young Black males with vocational classes. Along with a general education curriculum, the school offered courses in auto mechanics, blacksmithing, forging, foundry work, tailoring, electroplating, business, bookkeeping, secretarial work, cosmetology, and quality cooking. The school was established with federal "New Deal" funds and was partly intended to support returning WWII veterans. In 1956, Don Thompson High School was demolished, and a new building was constructed. The new facility, named Howard W. Blake High School, was located west of the Hillsborough River. While reviewing the history of Don Thompson School, I learned that the school was torn down before Blake was built, which might explain why we moved at that time. I also think my dad didn't want to live across the street from a jail, so that could have been another reason for our move. Of course, they didn't tell me that because I was too young to understand, and they probably never thought to explain why we were moving, but we did.

When we moved, I remember telling them I wanted a house with a store—I didn't know exactly what I wanted, but I knew I wanted something like that. Guess what? They found a house with a store attached. I vaguely recall the people who sold it to us—a name that's nearly forgotten now—who lived right across from the Southern Cross Mattress Factory on

Rome Avenue and Chestnut. There was also a feed warehouse on Rome, so making those changes was a little different. But I've been involved in education since I was a little girl, singing in school, and I knew the mattress factory made mattresses.

When Blake opened, my mom started the store, and my dad began teaching at Blake. My mom ran the store during the day, made sandwiches for people at the feed warehouse, and served them to the Mattress Factory workers and others coming in and out of the neighborhood. I still meet people who remember the oatmeal cookies sold last year—those cookies from Jack's, a well-known company that made cookies all the time.. That's what we liked, especially the Nehi Sodas, which definitely come from yesteryear—strawberry and grape flavors that everyone enjoyed and that were always available. Those are the memories we cherish.

Compared to the past, especially when he was a little boy, people are now talking about guns. My father had one; however, I only saw it on the 4th of July and New Year's, when we were allowed to shoot in the air to celebrate. The other time was when someone tried to break into our store, and he pulled out his gun to see who it was. As a child, I never knew where he kept it or where he retrieved it from. Seemingly, it should happen nowadays, but it doesn't seem to be kept out of reach of anyone, especially young folks.

August 2, 1945. We were having fun; it was great. My hat probably came from one of our many trips to Texas.

This is my birthday party with my little friends, and I believe that's Lorraine. We are posing next to my dad's car. It's black because he always said a black car is the best to have, and that Chevrolet is one of the best kinds of cars.

This was when I had a bigger birthday party with all my friends. I remember some of them: Lorraine Baker, Betty, and Bobby. There were others too; it might have been Maxine, but I'm not entirely sure about everyone. We had a great time, and again, this was in our yard. You can see the car in the background; it looks a bit older than the previous ones, but probably around the same age or a little older.

Yes, I was a party girl, so this looks like an older version of me standing there. Everywhere we went, we always dressed up, with your ribbon in my hair and cute little clothes. Of course, my parents did that; it was something my mother insisted on. She wanted me to always look nice.

Family Life

My parents visited Florida and traveled to various cities across the state. This might include Silver Springs, where we took a glass-bottom boat ride. I'm not certain, but they made sure to see different parts of Florida. So, again, this might not be exactly where I think it is, but they love to travel, and this could be a picture from anywhere in Florida. Orlando was another destination, and Jacksonville was important to me because we took my mom's friend there. You mentioned Jacksonville again. Daytona Beach was also on our list, and I recall visiting Fernandina Beach, where Black families owned properties and beachfront homes. I really enjoyed going there with my mother, her friend, and my dad.

I have a friend with me. My parents would invite one of our friends who had a little girl, and we would go on trips. Silver Springs is about as far as I think they would let her go with us, not because she was bad, but because parents at that time did not let their kids go everywhere with anyone, even if they were good friends. This appears to be a picture of me and Lorraine Baker.

Many people my age would recognize her because, I believe, her grandfather owned a bookstore. She spent a lot of time with them, along with her mother. I'm mentioning this is her because we went everywhere together. My parents often took her along with us because she was my little buddy at the time.

My parents knew Mrs. Walker, and we frequently visited her. Walker's Lake was one of the places Blacks usually went for swimming, besides Keystone. It was always very nice to visit Walker's Lake and have fun, especially with her two daughters, Janice and I can't remember the other one's name. It was always an enjoyable time to play there when my parents visited.

This is a picture of a club, but I don't remember its name. In the picture, Mrs. Alexander is visible; she had a goldfish pond in her yard. The other person at the very end, wearing glasses, looks like Mrs. Stephens, who lived on the next block on Morgan St. My mother is in the background, smiling, and I was trying to see if my daddy was holding me because he's always doing that. There's a small picture of me there, and this was one of the times they enjoyed—when everyone got together and always had a good time.

This is still the other part of the party we saw earlier, and I'm not sure if it's a club. Some of the people there were right here in the city, and some of you might recognize them if I can still remember their names. I'm not sure about the Christian man—this looks like daddy, but I'm not really sure because of how he's standing. Still, it was a nice little time, and of course, they carried me everywhere. There was no time I was at home or left with anyone else, and I always say fine.

Looking at this hat again, I believe it really came from Texas. They brought it for me, and I wouldn't have taken it off. The background shows what Scott Street and Morgan looked like—that's the store there. There were other houses on that street, but that's part of the scenery near our house. If you need to go to the store, it's just a short walk away. That's one of the things I really remember. Again, I don't remember who that person was, but I had friends named Betty and Bobby. You can see I look very happy and pleased with my little hat and the outfit my mom and dad bought for me.

The Scott Street store is visible in the background. We are standing on Morgan Street.

This shows the outside of the sidewalk. You saw the other one where you had to stay inside and not go out, but in this one, someone is probably watching me from the sidewalk. You can still see Miss Laurel's house in the background, which always looked very creepy. But again, this was just a location. The fence you're looking at stretched all the way down to Mrs. Stone's house at Stone's Funeral Home, which is much larger. I am standing at the corner of Morgan and Laurel streets.

LEFT: Site where our home once stood on Morgan Street.

BELOW: Site where Don Thompson once stood on Morgan Street.

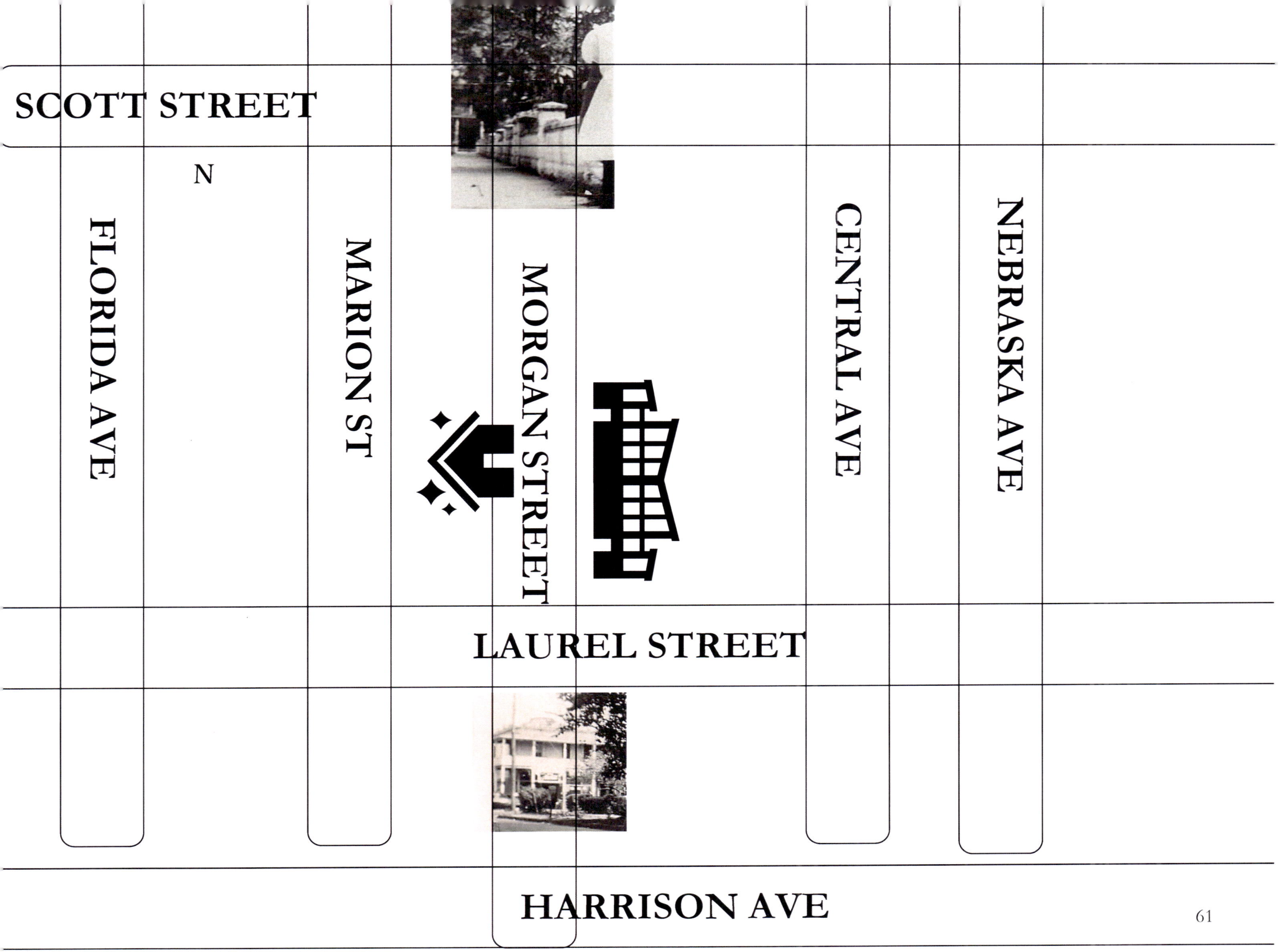

SCOTT STREET

N

FLORIDA AVE

MARION ST

MORGAN STREET

CENTRAL AVE

NEBRASKA AVE

LAUREL STREET

HARRISON AVE

This is Uncle Willie, my father's brother, who was from Longview, TX. He came to see what Florida was like, and this picture was taken on Bayshore, where it was so clean and pretty that they decided to take a picture of him there. I don't remember him staying very long when he came to Florida, but it was really great to have him here. I don't remember any other family members coming to Florida, but it was truly special to have him with us. As small as I was, I really enjoyed it.

Today, according to Wikipedia, Bayshore Boulevard is a waterfront road along Hillsborough Bay in South Tampa, Florida. Located south of downtown Tampa, the sidewalk is 4.5 miles long and 10 feet wide, and it is the second-longest continuous sidewalk in the United States, after Seawall Boulevard in Galveston, Texas. There is a 3-mile bike lane, a linear park, and the Bayshore Greenway Trail, which offers scenic views of urban Tampa and the water. The sidewalk features benches, a water fountain, bicycle parking, a city marina, and exercise stations.

This is a picture of Mr. and Mrs. Sheehy. Mrs. Sheehy wanted to ensure you pronounced her name correctly.

They often took someone to Rogers Park, stopping along the way at places where we could pick up items for a small picnic.

The tree in the background no longer exists. The cars were impressive. The dress Mrs. Sheehy is wearing is back in style—the floral print and simple design that we keep seeing in fashion. Once again, the ladies dressed up, even if it was just for a picnic.

This is a picture of me standing in Orlando at the tuberculosis hospital. We were there to visit a cousin, and in fact, we would make that trip at least once a week or every other week to see her.

She was also from Texas, and most people knew where it was. Constance Stephens, we Stephens were during that time. Now, I don't even know if this is all still in place—the Orlando tuberculosis hospital is there, but that's me standing there, posing and looking neat.

According to *Florida Memories,* the hospital was a P.W.A. project known as the Central Florida Tuberculosis Hospital, the Sunland Training Center for Retarded Children, and the Sunland Hospital of Orlando. It was dedicated in 1938 and located at 7500 West Silver Star Road. It was destroyed in 1999 after years of disuse following the mid-1980s closure of the Sunland hospitals of Florida.

Howard, Alice, and unknown

It looks like this is in Longview, TX, with my cousin. I've always liked my older cousin Howard. We had several cousins there; this is probably one of them is the little boy sitting with us. For some reason, I remember his name.

Every year, whether it was after school, during summer, or at Christmas, we would go to Longview, which I always thought of as a small country town, and I still believe that. As a little girl, though, it felt very different from what I was used to in Tampa and in Marshall, TX, a college town where my mom lived. In this picture, I thought it was something really special. We'd go every year, and one year my dad wanted me to see them kill a hog. I thought that was the worst thing. I do remember that, and another thing was picking corn. I've never liked dirt. I don't know how my cousins probably felt about that, and I might have seemed like a little spoiled brat compared to the work they had to do.

I remember asking my oldest cousin, Howard, if I could come in. I think he was churning butter or doing something similar, and I asked if I could join him.

The kitchen was just outside the window where they were processing the hog, and I refused to look at it. I thought that was the worst thing to see. But that was an experience my dad wanted me to have, and so was being in the cornfield. Again, I never liked dirt, and I didn't want to be involved in so many different things. You have to hang out when the person was telling me that. My dad had two brothers, so Uncle Hayman was the one with all the kids. It could have been my dad, Uncle Hayman, and my granddad doing this terrible thing, which I thought was about killing. That was something accessible to everyone, and I understand it was for survival. For everyone, that was your bacon and other essentials needed at the time. My experience was mainly visiting them, and since I am more of a city person, I thought it was okay to go, but to me, that was really the countryside.

One of the oldest girls was from Milan. Regarding her illness, there was someone named Kadel. I had never seen anyone with disabilities before, and you don't see many now. She had a disproportionately large head, and they made her sit in a chair all the time. I don't know what that's called now, and I don't even know if she was born that way. I always thought that was one of the strangest things to see—someone like that. I do remember her name was Kadel. All of these experiences either happened during Christmas after school was out or at the end of summer when we took that drive from Texas to Tampa for Christmas. It was either during Christmas or summer. We would go to Marshall, Texas, first, which is on my mom's side of town. Her sisters and brothers lived there. Again, Marshall was a college town, so it felt more like a city, and I was used to the smaller town here, so it seemed okay to go there. I guess I might sound prejudiced saying that, but my experience and time just made it look different. Now, I've gone to Texas since then; everyone on my mother's side has passed away, and thanks to them, the only one left on that side is her immediate family. Another cousin passed away about three years ago, and I'm the only one left on the Stephens side of the family. On my dad's side, the Moore side, there are four surviving members.

Over time, I've visited them a few times for their Labor Day get-togethers, and we've stayed in touch at different points. Believe it or not, there's another cousin with the same name as mine, except my middle name is Marie. Marie was the name I was given, named after my cousin on my mother's side of the family.

When I got married, my grandmother was named Alice, so I was Alice Roberts. Can you believe it? When my parents had my dad, grandma, and granddad's wedding license, my grandmother's maiden name was Roberts.

Imagine how far back that goes—the marriage license is really old, as old as the hills. It was a long time ago, so I suppose my mom named me Alice. My cousin, who's a little older, also shares the same name, Alice Moore, except my middle name is Marie (after Cousin Constance Marie Stephens Horton).

Don Thompson Vocational School

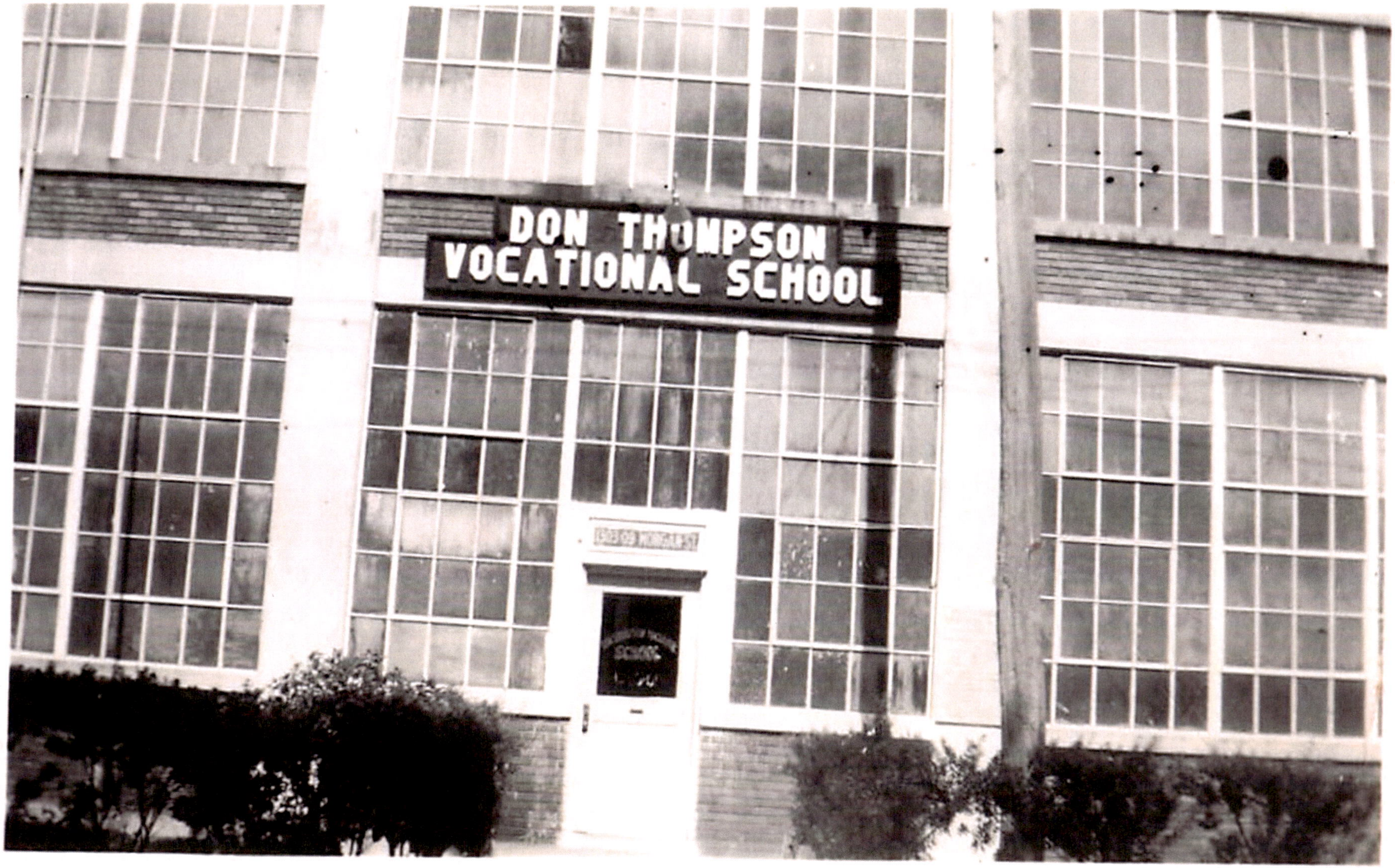
DON THOMPSON
VOCATIONAL SCHOOL

This is the front of Don Thompson, and just think, my dad taught welding there. All he had to do was walk right across the street to go to work, which was definitely a convenience. Looking at the school photo now, it's amazing because I thought that was a brand-new building that looked fantastic, especially considering how small I was.

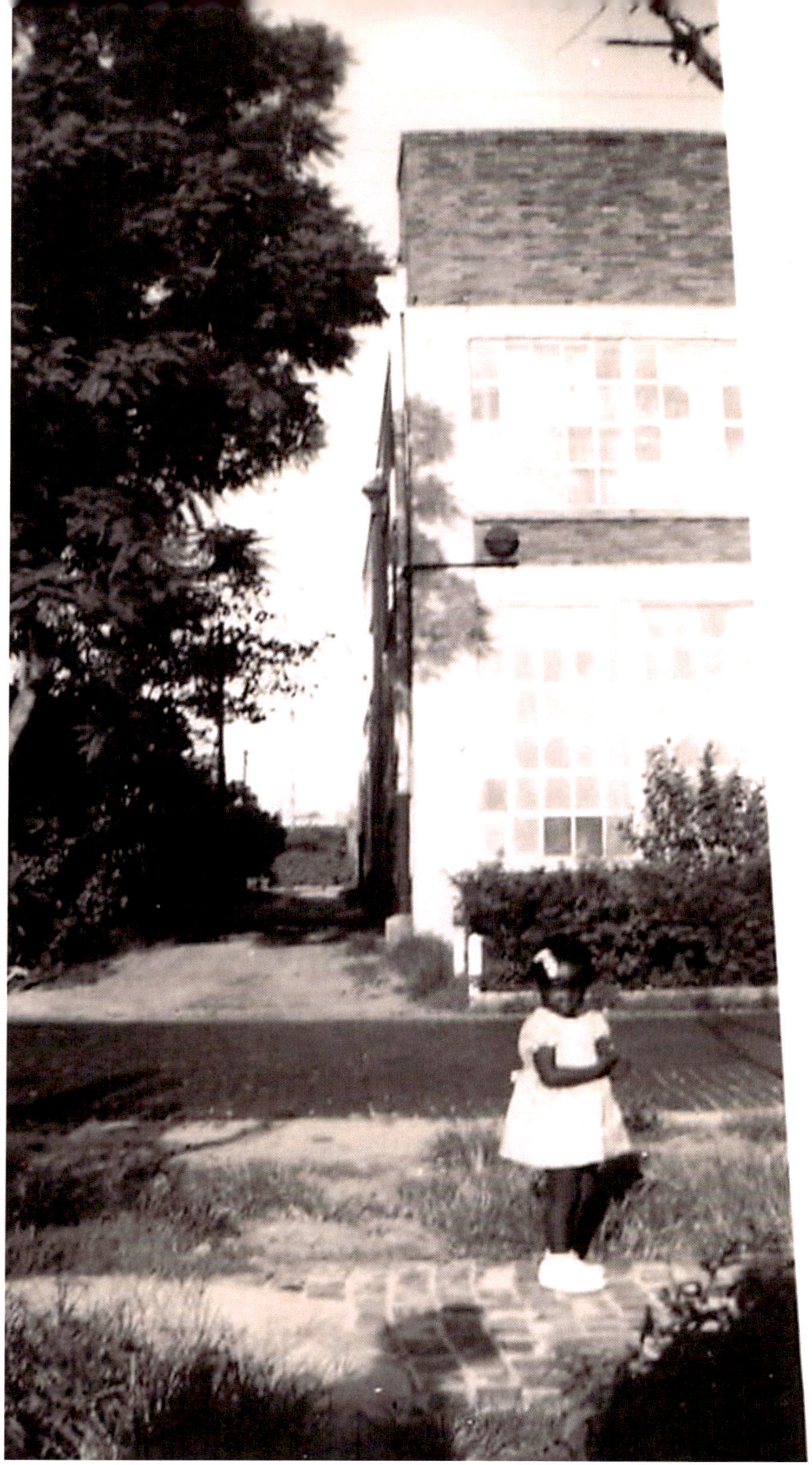
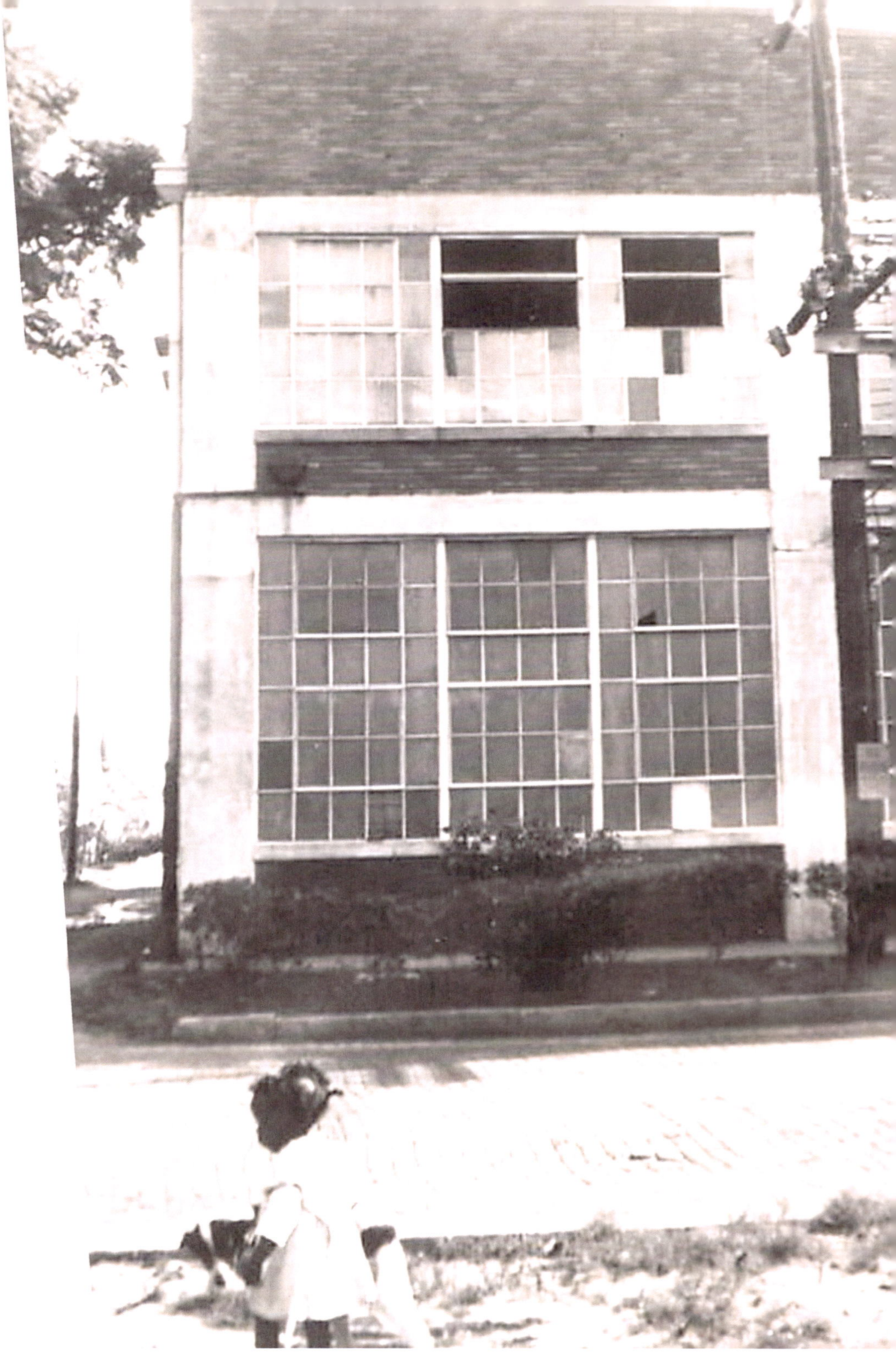

In these pictures, I'm playing in the yard right across from Don Thompson High School. The small part of the alley is where people from Central Park, some from Floribraska, and others from all around Tampa would gather. I mention West Tampa, Central Park, and Belmont Heights—you should come and play basketball and roller-skate there. They used that alley, which was between Mrs. Alexander's house, where you saw me sitting at the fishpond. Everyone used that alley on weekends and during the week to play basketball and roller skate.

In this view of Don Thompson, you can see all those trees right where the alley used to be in the back.

For us, the focus was on the black car, and Dad always made sure it was a Chevrolet. I never forget that, even though I didn't get a similar car when I bought one. That was definitely drilled into me.

In front of the school, which you can see directly from our house, there were houses all up and down that block.

This picture of Daddy was possibly taken in Tallahassee or Texas. From the left, he's first in the back row. If it's Tallahassee, it would be FAMU, where he taught a welding class. If it's in Texas, it would be where he finished school and taught. He was a graduate of Prairie View A & M University, a former welding instructor at FAMU, and retired from the Hillsborough County School Board.

Introducing my book to Mrs. Dawson, the curator of FAMU's Meek Eaton Black Archives, proved to be thrilling. She discovered that my father was indeed at FAMU in 1944 and left shortly thereafter for Tampa, FL to live and teach at Don Thompson. This revealed that my mother, based on my calculation, was pregnant when they moved from FAMU to Tampa. That was new information to me.

Upon hearing about visits to the Crump family, Mrs. Dawson informed me about Tallahassee's Crump Brothers. They were from a family of landowners who also owned a bar. We have not verified that this family is the same as the famous Ben Crump family. However, we strongly believe there is a connection. I do know the Crump family we visited was either our great friends or possibly family.

What tickles me is Daddy standing there looking just like me. I know I look like "him" since he's the master copy!

Here you see Don Thompson and a scene from the welding class showing Daddy and students at work. On the right, wearing goggles and overalls, is my dad, teaching the class or demonstrating how to operate the welder. I have met many former welding students who remember him well. I believe he really enjoyed this because when he first came to Florida, he also taught welding at FAMU, which was then a combined vocational school and college. Moving to Tampa allowed him to get a job he loved, and he could just walk across the street to work, which was perfect.

The welding class is taught by Mr. Moore, who is sitting in the center of the photo. All his students who learned welding from him are in the picture. Some of them might also have learned to drive from him, but I'm not sure because they seem a bit younger. I still cross my legs just like he does whenever I sit down. This is his dad and his welding experience.

This is a picture from the welding class, showing everyone in their helmets and outfits. Daddy is sitting on the floor right in front of everyone. This was one of those times when they said I used to go back and forth through the classroom, so I guess this time they made sure I didn't appear in front of it. But this is his class, and I don't know what year this was.

A photo of the teachers at Don Thompson; some of them I remember. Mr. Gren'on was young and stood in the front row on the left. Mr. Sheehy was there, along with Mr. Boston. Mr. Sheehy was a landscaper, and Mr. Gren'on taught tailoring. I don't remember what Mr. Boston did. There are some others, like Moses Powell, Mr. Pride, Mr. Bexley, and Mr. Duhart, Coach Williams, and Mr. Boston, that I don't quite recognize.

I also remember seeing a couple of ladies who I believe were secretaries. There was only one lady who taught cosmetology. You know how memory fades with time, but she was one of the people who taught cosmetology. All these people taught different trades, and this was the staff. Some of them were dressed in ways you don't see anymore, like wearing dresses and bow ties, which was something new, especially in school. Now you don't see any of that anymore.

This looks like a teacher training class, with Daddy sitting cross-legged and wearing socks, or maybe he is the man sitting behind him. The stovepipe in the background shows how old this setting is. You no longer see that kind of pipe in classrooms or buildings. Air conditioners now dominate the scene.

Did you notice the woman in the third row by the window?

Today, some younger folks will probably laugh out loud, while some older folks will pretend that they don't notice what the car looks like. This car was a classic at the time. Dad loved it because he also taught in driver's ed, and that car stayed in front of our house. Therefore, we had two cars, our black Chevrolet and a white driver's ed car.

In fact, he taught me how to drive and parallel park. He also tried to teach me how to drive a stick shift, but I just couldn't get the hang of it. That was one of his other areas of expertise: welding, driver's education, and auto mechanics.

Ferman Chevrolet Co. apparently had a relationship with the school. Today, according to its website, the Ferman family of dealerships is a local, family-owned and operated business based in Tampa, FL. Established in 1895, they grew from a bicycle shop to serve Hillsborough, Pinellas, and Pasco counties, with multiple dealership locations representing 12 new-vehicle brands. In 2019, they introduced FORCE Customs.

They are the seven[th]-largest automobile dealer in the United States and have received the NADA Century Award, which honors America's car dealers that have been in business for 100 years or more. They are currently approximately 130 years old.

Middleton, Don Thompson, and Blake

Middleton High School was in East Tampa. Don Thompson and Blake High School were in downtown Tampa. All three schools served predominantly Black communities.

Don Thompson served as both a vocational school and a high school. When Blake High School was built, Don Thompson was regarded as the vocational and high school option, whereas Middleton was preferred because it operated more like a college-preparatory high school.

After they closed Don Thompson and Blake, some of their trade programs were eliminated. Don Thompson offered tailoring, brick masonry, welding, and landscaping. Middleton, however, was solely for college-bound students and traditional high school students. If students wanted to learn a trade, they would attend other schools.

When the school moved to West Tampa, it was renamed Howard W. Blake in honor of Mr. Howard Wesley Blake. Later, some trade programs like cosmetology, brick masonry, and vocational auto mechanics were removed. In the past, my dad taught there at night, but that changed, which led to the removal of some trades because welding was no longer offered, nor was tailoring. They also cut landscaping and related programs. Blake no longer had those. They might have considered downsizing or simply decided not to include those programs anymore. I don't know.

Blake was also a high school. I started there in 7th grade. Most students on the West Side of town, including those from the Citrus Park area in Tampa and Port Tampa, went to Blake High School. Students on the East Side went to Middleton. My parents—my dad was a die-hard Rattler and a die-hard Yellow Jacket. As I got older, I met Mrs. Sheehy, a teacher and my parents' friend. She liked to pronounce her name 'She,' and you had to say it that way. She asked if I could spend a day working with her at

Middleton and staying there. I don't remember what subject she taught—could have been English or history. I fell in love with Middleton, of course, and, being the only child, I insisted on transferring to there. My dad and mom reluctantly agreed.

So, I'm still called a traitor by the Blake people, and I haven't lost that label. Of course, I don't remember talking to Middleton, so that's just some of the things that were there and how time and life affected us all at this age. We still remember the good times and how our environment has changed. I ran into people who remember my mom's store, and I was getting ready to take my first cruise when someone recognized me from the oatmeal cookies at Jacks, which no longer exists. I had a computer teacher who lived a few blocks down and described my mother's store, talking about the cookies and drinks back then. Over time, I kept running into people—many remember the store, and some recall my father from Don Thompson. One of the guys I attended church with talked about me, remembered being in school, and described how children from various neighborhoods came to play basketball and roller skating. These are different times that the people still living remember, although many have now passed away.

A Many people still remember me as a little girl, and many remember my name. I know many of them through my mom's social life, and my dad was involved as well. She went out more than he did, and I never understood why she never learned how to drive. He told drivers, "Yeah, she never learned." I don't know. I guess she just got used to him driving. Oh well, nothing was lost, but he left, and she never learned to drive.

Social Life

These are pictures from when they used to hold teas and fundraisers. Everyone is here, and you'll notice that everyone is wearing hats except for two people: Miss Perry and someone else who may live with her. My mother is in the background next to her, by the wall, wearing her black hat. It looks like... oh, I forgot the tycoon's name, but Miss Lomas is standing next to me. I'm the little person with my bow on. Miss Lomas is one of the people, and Ida Stephens lived on the next block from us, near Don Thompson, and on Morgan Street.

The other person is Miss Alexander, who had the goldfish pond right next door, which separated her yard from the alley between Don Thompson's yard and hers. These were often the little teas and activities they held to raise money. I'm not even sure how they did it, but I know you all would remember having tea books when you used to go around collecting for the teas they hosted. Being dressed and in style, I want to make sure I'm not left behind in all this. Noticing the Easter Bunny, no doubt this tea was for Easter.

Tea books might seem old-fashioned, but years ago, they were little books where you would sign your name and make a donation—regardless of the amount. Then, people would go around, or I should say, some members of the club would do this. It was mostly just a way to collect donations, and people would give whatever they had for tea. They had small cards—well, not exactly carbon paper, but something similar—that they would cut and decorate for use. They made sure everyone had them, and it was no problem if you asked or mentioned that you had a tea book. It was simply a part of our culture growing up, and I'd say it was something our culture invented during that time.

The tea books were made from construction paper. I couldn't remember the name of the material before, and they would cut it out. I don't recall whether they were stapled together, but I do remember they would put a little ribbon on them and tie them together. I'm not sure about the different decorations they used all over, and I guess everyone decided on their own little section to focus on. This was something really unique. I never got to go out and make these myself, but other kids did. They would do that for the team.

Back Row: 3rd from left is Mary Moore (Mom), Mrs. Alexander, Alice (me)
Seated: Mrs. Pughsley, Mrs. Williams (mother of two doctors), Mrs. Walker

A club, and once again, I never knew the names of any of the clubs my mother was involved with. From left to right, there are two people whose names I don't remember. Miss Alexander, whom you've heard me mention, with her house and little pond. Of course, that's me standing there, looking all innocent. Sitting down are Mrs. Pughsley, Mrs. Williams (two doctors as son), and Mrs. Walker. Mrs. Walker is related to Reverend Jimmy Howell, and next to her is Miss Williams, who is Doctor Williams, Mrs. Williams's mother. I believe this is Miss Pughsley on the end, but I'm not sure. Again, you see I went everywhere; I never left and was right there with everyone. Miss Pughsley sits next to Miss Williams at the end of the sofa, and Miss Williams is in the middle on the left.

Standing: 4th from left is Mrs. Walker of Walker's Lake (Janis' mom), unknown, Ursula
Williams (Don Williams' mom)
Seated: Mrs. Alexander, Mrs. Williams

The club names escape me, but I remember the people and that they met together. To mention a few, Mrs. Williams married Dr. Williams, the husband of another Dr. Williams. I can't recall her name right now. The two other ladies, going from right to left, I'm not familiar with who they are. One is Mrs. Walker, and the other is Miss Walker, but I'm not sure which one is which. Then there's Mrs. Alexander, with Miss Alexander— oh, excuse me, let me backtrack. Ursula is also part of the Williams family; she is another Williams. I believe this is Mrs. Reddick, starting at the end and moving from right to left. I don't remember her name, and I think the person sitting next to her is Miss Pugsley, but I don't want to swear to that. I believe, again, that the mother is Mrs. Williams, the mother of Dr. Williams and Rishay Williams. I've forgotten the other Williams' name, but both were doctors. And again, there's Miss Alexander from Morgan Street and the pond.

West Tampa Teenage Club 40 + 50's: North Blvd Homes

Initially, I thought this group photo was from a graduation class, but I changed my mind when I saw there were no caps and gowns. So, this might have been a dance we attended in our younger days when they organized special events for us. It was taken on North Blvd., and surprisingly enough, you wouldn't guess that by looking at how things are today. But you can see everyone in their gowns and the guys in their little suits; that was a trend back then. Of course, we always had a great time, and there was nothing to worry about. Mom, Dad, and all the instructors and teachers would set it up right there, and we always had a blast. Trusting the captions, this is the West Tampa Teenage Club from North Blvd Homes.

This was an event they attended and enjoyed. Dad is standing in the background wearing a black jacket, and I'm sitting in front with my mom, who, as we say, never left home without taking us along. So, I was involved in everything and everywhere, but I'm not sure what the gathering was for; it might have been a luncheon. You can also see the men behaving well, just like the little kids in their places.

Scribed on the back of the photo was "Richedene told me to send you a photo. She was glad to see you, James & Marie." A relative on my mother's side of the family.

About The Author

Alice Moore, author of Alice Moore's Family Album

Memories of Don Thompson Vocational High School inspired Alice's dedication to public service and community empowerment. Alice is the daughter of James Henry Moore, the beloved teacher at Don Thompson Vocational High School, and she grew up directly across the street from the school. As a result, her roots are deeply connected to the school's history. Alice's career spans more than 50 years in public service, including 30 years with The Florida Department of Labor and Training Programs as a Community Service Worker with the WIN (Work Incentive) Training Program and as an Employment Specialist, and 15 years as a recruiter for the Job Corps Training Programs. In 1967, she began as a clerk in the community voting office and, for four years, collaborated with Carig Latimer at Hillsborough County's Supervisor of Elections on local, state, and federal elections, managing various precincts. Alice has worked and volunteered for candidates at all levels to register voters, inform the community, and encourage participation. She has volunteered with Urban Alliance and currently volunteers with Florida Rising. She remains committed to fostering community growth and passionately seeks to preserve her community's legacy, including Don Thompson Vocational High School.

Moore Life & Love

Alice Moore